37th International System Safety Conference 2019

Norfolk, Virginia, USA
29 July – 2 August 2019

ISBN: 978-1-7138-0948-7

Printed from e-media with permission by:

Curran Associates, Inc.
57 Morehouse Lane
Red Hook, NY 12571

Some format issues inherent in the e-media version may also appear in this print version.

Printed with permission by Curran Associates, Inc. (2020)

For permission requests, please contact International System Safety Society
at the address below.

International System Safety Society
P.O. Box 70
Unionville, Virginia 22567-0070
USA

Phone: 540-854-8630

systemsafety@system-safety.org

Additional copies of this publication are available from:

Curran Associates, Inc.
57 Morehouse Lane
Red Hook, NY 12571 USA
Phone: 845-758-0400
Fax: 845-758-2633
Email: curran@proceedings.com
Web: www.proceedings.com

TABLE OF CONTENTS

System Safety & Security: Establishing a Holistic Assurance Process for Safety-critical Systems

Braun Claudia, B.Sc.; Frequentis AG; Vienna, Austria

Gerstinger Andreas, Dipl.-Ing. Dr.; Frequentis AG; Vienna, Austria

Schedl Gabriele, Dipl.-Ing.; Frequentis AG; Vienna, Austria

Keywords: safety and security, co-assurance procedure, safety process, risk assessment, safety-critical systems

Abstract

The integration of security measures into a well-founded safety assurance process is a growing demand in the domain of safety-critical systems. In many cases, the safety assurance procedures are well-established at companies. Even to tie in the most necessary security actions already present a major challenge. This paper deals with the first steps to setup a viable procedure to (co-)assure systems' safety and security at Frequentis AG, primarily in the sector of air traffic management.

A research on the state of the art of co-assurance approaches has been conducted: existing analysis and risk evaluation methods, proposed procedures of certain certification standards, as well as novel approaches like the Safety-Security Assurance Framework. Furthermore, Frequentis' internal procedures, needs and (pre)conditions have been evaluated. Based on this research, a concept for a suitable co-assurance process has been developed. Additionally, interfacing gates during system development and handovers in system operation between the safety and security specialists of Frequentis have been created and already practiced.

The results of this work can be used as an approach for a stepwise integration of security objectives into an existing safety assurance infrastructure to improve the safety management system.

Managing Unit Tests Using Vector Spaces

Anthony S. Cantone; Naval Air Warfare Center Weapons Division (NAWCWD);
China Lake, California, US

Erica Arroyo; Naval Air Warfare Center Weapons Division (NAWCWD);
China Lake, California, US

Keywords: Unit Tests, Underlying Vector Spaces, Basis Sets

Abstract

Unit tests furnish assurance of error free operation of code modules, enhancing safe operation of code-intensive systems. The underlying vector space of a structured code module can be used to construct a minimal set of unit tests if a basis set of such a vector space can be found. This paper explores the use of basis sets to design a minimal set of unit tests and demonstrates how a basis set of tests is adequate for a logical test of a module containing a multitude of paths of execution.

Overview of ISO/PAS 21448: Road Vehicles - Safety of the Intended Functionality

Rami Debouk, Ph.D.; General Motors Company; Warren, MI, USA

Keywords: Safety, Intended Functionality, Road Vehicles

Abstract

The importance of safety in the development of safety-critical automotive systems has been increasingly growing, especially with the introduction of integrated driver assist and automated driving systems. The ISO 26262: Functional Safety –Road Vehicles Standard defines safety as the absence of unreasonable risks arising from malfunctioning behavior of the system. However, for some systems potentially hazardous behavior can be caused by the intended functionality, for instance due to a sensor performance limitation. The latter is referred to as the Safety Of The Intended Functionality or SOTIF, and has been introduced by the recently published ISO/PAS 21448.

This paper gives an overview of the ISO/PAS 21448. SOTIF by definition deals with the absence of unreasonable risk resulting from functional insufficiencies or due to reasonably foreseeable misuses. Guidance on the applicable design, verification and validation measures needed to achieve SOTIF are discussed. This includes the system specification, identification and evaluation of hazards caused by the intended functionality, and any modifications needed to reduce the risk due to SOTIF. In addition, the verification and validation strategy and activities are discussed as well as the method to accept the residual risk following the SOTIF activities. The expectation is that ISO PAS/21448 is complementing the safety activities performed while following ISO 26262.

Finally, this paper introduces the timeline to publish an international standard on SOTIF, ISO 21448.

Is AI in Healthcare Doomed, or Destined for Greatness?

Bijan Elahi; Medtronic; Eindhoven, The Netherlands

Keywords: artificial intelligence, AI, medical device, safety, ISO 14971

Abstract

Fully automatic and autonomous medical systems are already released and being used. Nurses and doctors have started adopting the technology to reduce manual work, and to provide more accurate service and impactful interventions to patients. Increased access, better outcomes, reduced costs and more personal and customized healthcare are the promise of AI. But unlike other commercial systems where performance is paramount, in healthcare, patient safety is the primary concern. There is a tremendous drive to capitalize on AI capabilities as soon as possible and as much as possible. However, there is a risk to AI's success. People expect infallibility from AI – far more than they expect from human physicians. As a result, only a few catastrophic events involving AI could spell doom for AI in healthcare.

Applying Safety Concepts and Principles in Vital Controller Design

Fenggang Shi, PhD; Thales Canada Transportation Solutions; Toronto, Canada

Keywords: safety critical system, vital controller, safety concepts, CBTC,

Abstract

A vital controller is safety critical and its failures, if not mitigated in time, can contribute to hazards in the application system. With electronics advancing and automation increasing, the expanding complexity of a vital controller creates challenges in its design and assessing its safety integrity level. Typically, traditional safety engineering approaches are not effective for providing systematic guidance to design vital controllers and also not cost efficient for justifying their safety integrity. Through practice on developing multiple Communications-Based Train Control systems, we have identified an approach to using a set of safety concepts as guidance for both safety critical controller design and its safety integrity assessment. These safety concepts are categorized as intrinsic fail-safe, reactive fail-safe, and composite fail-safe. An effective combination of them is applying the composite fail-safe concept in checked redundancy techniques for designing the architecture of a controller, the reactive safety concept for identifying self-testing and monitoring mechanisms in each checked redundant channel, and the intrinsic fail-safe concept for ensuring safe interfaces to other controllers and controlled devices. This paper presents the approach for using these safety concepts and discusses their application principles and verification factors for achieving high safety integrity level of a controller.

Concept and Development of a Science, Engineering, & Technology Student (SETS) System Safety Challenge Program

Lee Wayne Flint, BS Civil Engineering; The Olde Tinkerer LLC; Lucedale, MS, USA

Keywords: Science Engineering & Technology Students, Concept, Guidance & Criteria Handbook, Challenge

Abstract

This paper addresses the idea and concept development of a program to challenge Science, Engineering, and Technology Students (SETS) to incorporate a system safety component into their science and engineering fair projects. This concept development initiative was undertaken by the Virtual Chapter of the International System Safety Society (ISSS) to address a lack of criteria or guidance to assist local ISSS Chapters in promoting and and/or judging science and engineering fair projects in terms of system safety. Expectations are that such a program would be sponsored by the ISSS and its member Chapters.

The development of the project concept has taken the form of a "Guidance and Criteria Handbook". The handbook would provide fair organizers an "all inclusive" source for the essential information, guidance, criteria, and basic system safety teaching aids necessary to successfully incorporate system safety into student project competitions. Further, it would provide the ISSS and its member Chapters the essential guidance and criteria for assisting fair organizers, sponsoring awards, mentoring, and judging the system safety component of the student projects. It will be noted that the program is not intended as a project "safety" program – it is specifically intended as a "system safety engineering" exercise.

Most importantly, incorporating system safety concepts and processes into SETS science and engineering fair projects will: introduce aspiring young engineers, scientist, and technologist to the system safety engineering discipline and profession; and, encourage participants to actually employ basic system safety methodologies and techniques in the concept and design phases of their projects.

System Safety: A Beginners Perspective

Daniel J. Foito; Sikorsky, A Lockheed Martin Company; Stratford, CT, USA

Keywords: Recruitment, Retainment, Training, Mentoring

Abstract

In academia, System Safety is not a well-known field. When the word "engineering" is mentioned, words that come to mind are design, innovation, progression, but not safety. This can be said for many high school and college engineering curricula, as most do not have a focus on safety. The primary focus is on technical design and the design process. System Safety is a growing field and will require more highly skilled and knowledgeable individuals in the future as system designs become more complex. In addition to the lack of focus in the academic community, much of the current expertise will be leaving the industry as many System Safety engineers will be retiring in the years to come. This paper provides experiences, impressions, and personal anecdotes regarding my career as a rookie system safety engineer. Topics include the training, mentoring, and other resources that were provided to me as well as what I would have preferred to be exposed to as I began my career. The goal is to initiate a discussion with management about providing ways to attract and retain new talent. This paper will recommend ways to accomplish this task as well as provide an example as to how I have begun doing this.

Learning from Creeping Changes

Zsuzsanna Gyenes, Ph. D. ; IChemE Safety Centre; Rugby, Warwickshire, United Kingdom

Keywords: creeping changes, management of change, major incidents (Joshua M. Paiz, APA Headings and Seriation, 2018)

Abstract

Past tragic events such as the fatal explosion and crash of Nimrod XV230, Space Shuttle Challenger or Columbia disasters, SHELL Moerdijk explosion, Herald of Free Enterprise, Kings Cross fire, and Texas City refinery explosion occurred in entirely different areas or industry sectors. There is, however, an aspect which is common in these cases, namely the phenomenon known as creeping change. The IChemE Safety Centre has recently addressed this topic, presenting a case study in its quarterly publication, the Safety Lore. They also provided practical tips to managers, process safety engineers, supervisors, and operators of industrial sites to learn how such major incidents involving creeping changes can be avoided. This paper demonstrates the phenomenon of creeping changes via two case studies from two different sectors. In addition, it suggests lead metrics associated with these events to help monitor the changes. Finally, it provides ideas to managers, supervisors, process engineers, and operators of how to address those changes in their work.

Model Based Functional Safety for Complex Software Intensive Systems

37th International System Safety Conference 2019

July 29 - August 2, 2019

Barry Hendrix, AS, BAAS, MBA; APT Research, Inc.; Huntsville, Alabama, USA

Keywords: functional safety, software safety, model based systems engineering

Abstract

Safety-Critical Systems and Safety-Critical Functions (SCF) must be the focus when conducting Functional Hazard Analyses and Functional Hazard Assessments (FHA). FHAs have become the prerequisite for software safety analysis since behavior of the software and systems must be well understood in the safety domain. Functional Safety models should focus on how the architecture and the physical system, the computer system, and embedded software contributions ensure correct and predictable system behavior. On complex systems with software intensive SCFs, in-depth software safety analyses must go beyond the traditional hazard analysis process of documenting summaries of severity, probability, risk and mitigation. Functional Safety should be the focus during detailed design and code level software safety analyses using various proven models and modern tools to depict the safety attributes in the design of various complex system architectures. Model Based System Engineering (MBSE) Functional Analyses and Functional Safety subsets should focus on the many complex interactions in software and functional failure and fault conditions and situations that can lead to hazards. Functional safety tasks as part of, and beyond, the FHAs and software safety analyses should be integrated into models producing Safety Use Cases, Safety Activity Diagrams, and Functional Flow Diagrams. These can influence and depict system and explicit safety requirements, design safety features, hazard mitigation, safety verification, and risk reduction actions in the design and operations leading to system certification. The end goal is to reduce the level of abstraction and depict safety attributes clearly with objective safety evidence in safety documentation to be used for approval and certification. Functional Safety can be implemented for various safety policies, methods, and best practices of different agencies, companies, and product lines.

Artificial Intelligence (AI) – the Need for New Safety Standards and Methodologies

Malcolm Jones, B.Sc., Ph.D., F. Inst. P., C.
Phys., C. Eng.; AWE; Aldermaston, Berks., UK,
RG7 4PR.

Keywords: Artificial Intelligence, machine decision making risk, new safety standards.

Abstract

There have been a series of challenges to develop appropriate safety standards and methodologies as technology evolves, to ensure their safe implementation. These challenges, which first arose at the dawn of the industrial revolution, will inevitably continue. New technologies will always seek to forge ahead in a competitive marketplace, failure to do so will inevitably lead to organisational demise. However, such developments must be matched by a complement of research activity seeking to ensure that appropriate new safety standards and methodologies are put in place to maintain acceptable levels of risk. A new challenge now confronts us in the form of artificial intelligence (AI) where we stand at the frontiers of decision making in relation to what roles machines and humans should play with regard to optimal decision making and how these impact on safety. These issues impact on organisations which propose AI application and those which are responsible for setting standards and regulation. This is the subject for discussion in this paper.

Hazard Considerations for Vulcan Centaur V Integrated Space Vehicle and Launch Vehicle Operations

Shawn M. Laabs; System Safety Manager; United Launch Alliance; Centennial, Colorado, USA

Gavin T. Campbell; System Safety Engineer; United Launch Alliance; Centennial, Colorado, USA

Jacob B. Dysart; System Safety Engineer; United Launch Alliance; Centennial, Colorado, USA

Dae S. Kim; System Safety Engineer; United Launch Alliance; Centennial, Colorado, USA

Stephen A. Seidl; System Safety Engineer; United Launch Alliance; Centennial, Colorado, USA

Lindsey A. Szabelski; System Safety Engineer; United Launch Alliance; Centennial, Colorado, USA

Keywords: Safety, Hazard, Space Vehicle, Launch Vehicle, Vulcan, Centaur V, Mission Integration

Abstract

Personnel safety is a major concern throughout integrated space vehicle and launch vehicle operations and testing; namely for the personnel that handle the launch vehicle and space vehicle. The hazard risks associated with integrated space vehicle and launch vehicle operations increases as the two vehicles are integrated together. These risks must be controlled to acceptable levels prior to the start of integrated operations. This paper will explore design controls for cranes and hoists, sling assemblies, hydrasets and loadcells, handling structures, flight hardware lift points, work platforms, RF emitters, non-ionizing radiation sources, hazardous materials, flight hardware pressure systems, ordnance systems, electrical and electronic systems, and seismic designs. This paper will also explore operational controls that must be in place after the designs have been finalized. Range Safety requirements, which are requirements levied by the US Air Force in order to conduct launch operations on a military installation, will be the catalyst of discussion for this paper as most launch operations occur on a military installation.

Missing Risk Factors of Automated Driving System

M Ito, NIL Software Corp.; 2-17-7 Kinuta Setagaya, Tokyo, Japan

Keywords: Safety, Autonomous Car, Concept phase, ISO 26262, SOTIF, DESH-G, Predictor

Abstract

We have to consider the various risk factors when considering automotive safety: for example, malfunction, imperfect environmental recognition, and security violation. We have standards to treat those hazard types: ISO 26262 (functional safety), ISO/PAS 21448 (SOTIF) and SAE J3061 (security), respectively. However, those risk factors don't cover all. We can distinguish the factors relating to the collaboration of multiple (Advanced Driver-Assistance Systems) ADAS or the difficulty of the decision of motion planner (Ito, 2018) (Ito, 2019a). In this paper, we provide the approach to identify the risk factors through analyzing the interface classes, that are communication between the environment-system, user-system, and system-system. We'll show the result of this analysis, and we believe this is useful for us to identify the hazard of the system from SAE level 2 to level 5.

(U) Ballistic Trajectory Calculations for an Extended Insensitive Munitions Hazardous Fragment Criterion

Kevin T. Miers, MS; US Army Armament Research, Development and Engineering Center; Picatinny Arsenal, NJ, USA

Daniel J. Pudlak, MS; US Army Armament Research, Development and Engineering Center; Picatinny Arsenal, NJ, USA

Brian E. Fuchs, Ph.D.; US Army Armament Research, Development and Engineering Center; Picatinny Arsenal, NJ, USA

(U) Abstract

(U) Currently, a 20J fragment projection curve is being used by the Insensitive Munitions (IM) community to distinguish between hazardous and benign energetic responses for various munition systems subjected to simulated combat threats. Substantial resources are being expended to obtain benign responses. Thus it is important for this criterion to be meaningful, accurate, and practical to use. The current criterion is often regarded as too conservative. Accordingly, efforts have been undertaken to devise an improved criterion for what a benign response should entail. Issues include intent of the curve, appropriate hazard metric, conditions at which the metric applies, how the criterion should vary for different shapes and materials, and how many fragments may violate the criterion. These ambiguities led to trajectory modeling being performed to reproduce the curve. It was found that the curve represents the maximum distance a chunky steel warhead fragment could travel with a 20J launch energy. An impact energy criterion would be desirable, but for smaller masses the hazardous distances become unbounded. The community decided to keep 20J as the hazard metric, but changed the criterion to 20J impact at 15m, with a different curves for several fragment densities. This curve guarantees that if the criterion is violated, a 20J impact would occur at 15m if the trajectory were lowered. Recently, there has been interest from other communities in extending the curve to cover 79J impacts at 15m, since 79J has long been viewed as a rule of thumb for lethal impacts. The authors have constructed the mass-distance curves being incorporated into this extended criterion. This paper documents the methodology and assumptions involved.

Model Based Systems Engineering for System Safety: An Introduction

Patrick R. Oliver, MAS; Lockheed Martin Missiles and Fire Control; Orlando, Florida, USA

Keywords: Architecture, Model-Based, Modeling, Requirements, MBSE, Systems Engineering, System Safety, Verification, Software, Functional Analysis

Abstract

Model-Based Systems Engineering (MBSE) has gained momentum as the predominant method of analyzing and deriving system requirements as well as verifying and validating system performance. Over the years, several frameworks have gained prominence as approved methods and formal techniques to model systems. MBSE technology continues to gain popularity and growth within the Systems Engineering domain, especially in the markets of complex systems. To remain relevant within the context of concurrent engineering, it is advantageous for system safety engineer to learn how these techniques are affecting system design so that safety is addressed within system development. This paper provides an overview of MBSE in theory and practice and provides high-level details on how the system safety engineer can utilize these methods to provide the most optimum impact for affecting safety design.

Evolution of the System Safety Engineering Discipline

Tom Pfitzer; A-P-T Research, Inc.; Huntsville, AL, USA

Keywords: System Safety Regulations, Risk Management, Safety Case

Abstract

As an engineering discipline, system safety engineering is relatively new, with an origin in the 1960s. During the last 60 years, the management approaches used by the discipline have evolved and six discrete ideas have come to the fore that can be characterized as phases or eras. The newer ideas have been implemented successfully by a few organizations, whereas the larger government sponsored system safety programs within the Department of Defense (DoD), NASA, and Department of Transportation (DOT) for the most part continue to use methods developed in the earlier eras. This paper describes the six eras, identifies their distinguishing features, and points to best practice documents that embrace and define each era, with focus on the risk management approach and the Safety Case.

But the Mishap wasn't my Fault: Including the Integration and Interoperability Fratricide Context in your Functional Hazard Analysis

Graham C. Pierson; MS Computer Science, BS Physics; NSWC; Dahlgren, VA USA

Keywords: integration, interoperability, fratricide, functional hazard analysis, system of systems

Abstract

A weapon system might cause unintended harm to its operators or their teammates. A system of complex weapon systems may produce the same undesired result. As our systems are integrated or interoperated as never before, hazard analyses must assess the risk inherent in this context. A safety practitioner can assess the system's contribution to a fratricide event outside the system boundary. Even if the other systems are necessary to realize such a mishap, is it even possible to define this contribution. The best assessment of Integration and Interoperability (I&I) Fratricide hazards will come from the system's safety program since these safety practitioners understand the system's hazards better than anyone else does. The Functional Hazard Analysis (FHA) identifies the system functions and safety hazards associated with functional failure. How could a safety practitioner use the FHA to assess system hazards in the I&I (Integration and Interoperability)context? This study will develop an I&I Fratricide FHA framework to efficiently assess system hazards related to potential mishaps that could be realized by functional interaction with another system.

Guidance on Test Item Configurations for Sympathetic Reaction Testing in Accordance with AOP- 4396

D. Pudlak, B. Fuchs

US Army Combat Capabilities Development Command - Armaments Center (CCDC-AC)

Picatinny Arsenal, NJ, USA 07806-5000

Email: daniel.j.pudlak.civ@mail.mil

Phone: (973) 724-2223

Abstract

To provide a review and guidance for properly selecting and constructing the appropriate configuration(s) for conducting the Sympathetic Reaction (SR) test per AOP-4396. This paper discusses the analyses conducted that identify the potential technical reasoning for the origins of the volumetric requirements found in STANAG-4396, which will be incorporated in AOP-4396 and can affect how the Sympathetic Reaction test is conducted when performing harmonized Insensitive Munitions and Hazard Classification testing.

The intention of this paper is to communicate, to the various Safety and Hazard Identification communities, the importance of the Sympathetic Reaction (Detonation) test, and the proposed origins of the requirements that bound the experimental test. The proposed origins of the requirements are discussed in this paper, and are theorized based on mathematical analyses that were conducted in reference to Standard NATO shipping and storage processes and materiel. The reader should better understand how to properly design the configuration, and set up the test item, for a Sympathetic (Reaction) Detonation test for Insensitive Munitions, Safety, and/or Hazard Classification/Division purposes. This test is an extremely valuable test to perform to understand / characterize the worst reaction a munition can produce when another adjacent munition detonates accidently. Performing and evaluating this test properly enables engineers to design IM Technology that provides a safer environment for Ammunition Load, Assemble, Package (LAP) Plant employees and the Warfighter.

System Safety Engineering Methodology Applied to High Voltage Automotive Battery Systems

Galen E. Ressler; General Motors Company; Warren, Michigan, USA

Keywords: high voltage battery safety, advanced automotive battery safety, lithium ion battery safety

Abstract

The high voltage battery systems in electric automotive vehicles are very complex and must balance many attributes such as performance, cost and timing while not compromising safety criteria. Among other things, a thorough and methodical approach to battery safety is necessary to achieve this balance. System safety engineering methodology provides such an approach and can be applied as a useful framework.

Potentially hazardous conditions related to functional safety (for example, charge control) as well as primary safety (for example, chemical and mechanical hazards) may both be addressed by applying such a system safety engineering methodology. Hazard identification and assessment, safety requirements development and definition, application of various safety analysis methods, and verification / validation activities are all part of this approach. Typical battery abuse testing, as well as newly defined limit testing, supports the effort.

Documentation, traceability and reviews provide a method to verify that all issues are addressed as well as providing a method to retain information for future reference. Specific examples provide insights to the application of the system safety process to systems which include both functional and primary safety hazards, useful to both new and experienced system safety practitioners.

Application of Divergence to Assess System Resilience Against Unforeseen Threats

J.R. Richardson, ESEP; Raytheon; Temecula, CA, USA

Keywords: divergence, resilience, unforeseen, threat, risk, mitigation

Abstract

Divergence theory and its practical application as an innovation exercise seeks to "open the aperture" and first expand the problem space, as opposed to just immediately converging toward a viable solution. This paper shares a use case application of a simple but powerful divergence methodology as an analytical technique to retire a major program critical risk believed by many to be technically impossible to address. The risk statement required system resilience against "critical omissions in the identification and classification of failure conditions, resultant hazards, and hazard severities." Many programs attack resilience by what-if-ing the problem until time and budget are exhausted and program leadership feels like due diligence has been served. But what else could be done to show resilience against truly unforeseen threats and critical omissions? Every time the what-if activity identifies a new threat it moves out of the unforeseen bucket into the known threats bucket. How do you prove resilience for everything that's still left in the unforeseen bucket – the things that nobody's ever thought of? This paper provides a method to do just that, and which was sufficient to retire the subject major program's critical omission risk.

Managing Industry Risk: Commercial Space Flight Safety Reporting

37th International System Safety Conference, July 29 - August 2, 2019

Timothy G. Riley, MS.; Sandia National Labs; Albuquerque, NM, USA

Keywords: analysis, FAA, reporting, safety, spaceflight, risk

Abstract

Human space transportation safety and risk management has evolved significantly over the sixty-plus years of strict oversight by the National Aeronautics and Space Administration (NASA). Beginning in the 1960s and driven primarily by Cold War motivations, the criticality of transparency and open reporting of safety concerns and potential areas of under addressed risk analysis have proven disastrous in high-visibility accidents such as the Apollo 1 fire, and the Space Shuttle Challenger and Columbia accidents. And now, both domestically and internationally, a commercial space industry is rapidly expanding, both for private consumption and in providing services to NASA and the U.S. military space complex. The new model of oversight, however, was built with the desire to rapidly grow the commercialization of space, counter to the slow, methodical, safety-based growth of the civil space programs of the past.

From a regulatory perspective, The Federal Aviation Administration, Office of Commercial Space Transportation (FAA/AST) is responsible for oversight of the commercial space industry. However, since the industry has become largely driven by entrepreneurial innovation and business models, Congress has written laws pertaining to the commercialism of space that ensure a non-intrusive approach, with an expectation that the industry be the one to develop and adopt consensus standards that evolve with the growth of space commercialism. Congress' vision was that commercial operators would develop industry-based safety excellence in their safety management programs and systems through a type of self-regulation. FAA/AST is responsible for regulating commercial space transportation operations only to the extent necessary to ensure public health and safety and the safety of property, with the ability of FAA/AST to enact regulations mandating safety management system requirements on commercial operators specifically limited to ensure that regulations do not hinder the development and growth of private space flight operators. Considering the FAA's limited role in oversight of commercial space operator safety, the emergence of the true private sector is shifting the role of the primary risk taker from the government (government as both the only launch provider and the primary customer) to private entities, in which the market bears the risk (government one of many customers). This rapid expansion of privatization in the launch, suborbital and orbital space markets, with minimal government oversight of safety, introduces unknown opportunities for incidents and accidents that may involve the public, private operator employees, and space flight participants (passengers). Of particular concern within the industry is how to prevent actions taken by one or two highly risk-tolerant launch providers that would adversely impact the industry as a whole. An industry-specific safety reporting system has multiple risk-reduction advantages, and conceptually can be developed alleviating concerns of over proprietary information. Much as NASA operates the Aviation Safety Reporting System (ASRS) for commercial aviation and the Confidential Close Call Reporting System (C3RS) for the railroads, these systems can be models for a safety reporting system that supports managing risks collectively, better ensuring the survivability of each operator by communicating openly amongst all operators. This paper will explore such a system for commercial space.

System Safety Semantics – The Use and Misuse of Terminology

Donald W. "Don" Swallom; United States Army Aviation and Missile Command; Redstone Arsenal, Alabama, United States of America

Keywords: semantics; definitions; risk; severity, probability; hazard

Abstract

In system safety practice a clear understanding of the terms we use helps us accurately assess and communicate risk in our endeavor of achieving the safety of systems, products and services. Terms that have been a source of confusion in the past include hazard, risk, causal factor, catastrophic, critical, negligible, marginal, criticality, acceptable, control, conservative, credible, failure condition, failure condition, source, mechanism and outcome. Some system safety practitioners use some of these terms a lot and some avoid them like the plaque. Some words like "hazard" have a variety of meanings depending on what industry they are used in. Some terms appear in some domains and are never used in others. Some terms are used by practitioners with a vague notion of their meaning and no sense of what they really mean. Miscommunication can be avoided by understanding that this can be a problem in communicating with other companies and domains, clearly defining terms and not assuming other practitioners have the same sense of a term as you do.

Harnessing Uncertainty in Autonomous Vehicle Safety

Stephen L. Thomas; Uber ATG; Pittsburgh, PA

Dirk J. Vandenberg; Uber ATG; Pittsburgh, PA

Keywords: autonomous, self-driving, safety case, uncertainty

Abstract

Safely developing self-driving vehicles presents technical challenges. Among the key technical challenges are how to confidently demonstrate the safety of a self-driving vehicle when the number of permutations of operating conditions, scenarios, system inputs, etc. are complex, uncertain, and potentially limitless. This paper provides a broad survey of the various types of uncertainty in the development of self-driving vehicles and will outline several possible strategies for handling uncertainty. Advantages and challenges of different approaches, including qualitative and quantitative methods, will also be discussed.

Addressing Multicore Risk for Firm and Soft Real-time Safety Critical Systems Gary D. Warren, PhD; SAIC; Reston, Virginia, USA Stuart Whitford, MS; BAH; Arlington, Virginia, USA Robert Alex; BAH; Arlington, Virginia, USA Keywords: Soft Real Time, Multi-Core Processing, Unmanned Systems Abstract Non-deterministic latency and jitter issues have arisen with the increased use of commercial multicore processors (MCP) as the hardware platforms for hosting Department of Defense (DoD) systems. Within the civilian world of avionics flight control, an approach to dealing with nondeterministic latency issues arising from interference channels within multicore-based, hard realtime, flight control applications has been documented in the Certification Authorities Software Team (CAST) Position Paper (CAST-32A) on Multi-Core Processors and the Federal Aviation Administration's report on Assurance of Multicore Processors in Airborne Systems (DOT/FAA/TC-16/51, dated July 2017). Many, perhaps most, DoD safety-critical systems are not hard real-time. Missing some deadlines can be tolerated and adequately addressed with mitigations such as data time-stamps and checks to discard "stale" data. As firm or soft real-time systems, performance may degrade, but catastrophic consequences can be prevented. For these systems, the approach used for hard realtime avionics flight control systems is unnecessary and not cost effective. This paper discusses the mismatch of the CAST-32A approach for firm and soft real-time, nonavionics systems and presents a simpler, more agile, testable approach to MCP risk control based on a long-used criterion from the realm of network management.

The Safety Culture of Your Organization: Considerations That Relate to Your System Safety Program

David B. West; Board of Certified Safety Professionals; Indianapolis, IN, USA

Abstract

Recently, the importance of safety culture has been studied, discussed, and written about extensively. Safety culture is the product of values, attitudes, perceptions, competencies, and behavior that determine the commitment to, and the proficiency of, an organization's health and safety management. Safety culture is often considered in the context of protecting the organization's employees, which relates to industrial safety. In this context, the need for safety culture is well understood and relatable to the organization, since their members benefit. Safety cultures of system safety organizations share some aspects with their industrial safety counterparts; however, many aspects differ, since system safety aims to ensure safety throughout the system's life cycle, and therefore, beneficiaries include not only production facility workers, but also the end users (customers, operators, passengers, etc.), as well as the general public and the environment. When implementing a system safety program, an organization should ensure that a strong, positive safety culture pervades the organization. Without a positive safety culture, the system safety practitioner's work is burdened, and the system safety effectiveness is reduced. In a strong safety culture, the entire team, including designers, developers, system engineers, testers, quality, configuration control, and management are all constructively contributing to system safety.

The Safety Challenge of Unmanned Autonomous Lethal Weapon Systems

Stuart Whitford, MS; BAH; Arlington, Virginia, USA Douglas Bower, MS; NOSSA; Indian Head, Maryland, USA Robert Alex; BAH; Arlington, Virginia, USA

Keywords: Unmanned Weapon Systems, Human-in-the-Loop, Machine Learning

Abstract

As the scope and range of unmanned lethal weapon systems grow, the requirement to maintain effective human control authority over ever-growing autonomy in the functionality allocated to the system's software becomes more and more challenging. Ensuring necessary human-in-theloop or on-the-loop control authority under greater and greater separation in space and time requires increasing attention to the design of the right redundancies in hardware, software, communication, and data through the entire infrastructure involved in mission command and control. Adding to these challenges is the mounting challenge of machine learning allocated to more and more of the software functionality that comprises the mission architecture for unmanned weapon systems. This paper provides an overview of this constellation of challenges and some of the means being employed to address them.

Strategy for Overcoming Regulatory and Technology Gaps to License Ground Transportation at the Speed of Sound in an Agile and Global Business Environment.

Jeff Williams, BSEE, Senior Safety Analyst; Hyperloop Transportation Technologies, Culver City, CA, 90230, USA

Key Words: Transportation, technology, collaborative regulation, pacing problem, hyperloop

Background

Hyperloop is the next revolution in mass transportation. It will be no less impactful than commercial air or high-speed rail (HSR). Design objectives include speeds near Mach one, net positive photovoltaic power, a high quality experience combined with convenience and moderate cost. Simply put, it will become a game changer in the densely populated areas it serves. This transportation revolution also poses system life-safety design challenges on par with manned space flight and nuclear submarines. When successfully commissioned, Hyperloop will represent a mode of transportation not envisioned by current transportation or business regulations. Hyperloop development efforts will build on CENELEC certification standards for railway safety to close regulatory gaps. Where there is no regulatory precedence, Hyperloop Transportation Technologies (HTT), other Hyperloop companies and industry partners must exceed current transportation safety levels using a robust design process that excels in system safety engineering. This is a business imperative in order to sustain both financial market and public confidence in Hyperloop as a beneficial undertaking.

AUTHOR INDEX

International System Safety Society
P.O. Box 70
Unionville, Virginia 22567-0070
USA

ISBN 978-1-7138-0948-7
9 781713 809487

CURRAN ASSOCIATES INC.
proceedings.com